Unbelievable Pictures and Facts About Siberian Huskies

By: Olivia Greenwood

Introduction

The Siberian Husky dog breed is a magnificent breed of dog. These dogs are highly intelligent and are often compared to wolves. Today you will be learning about this incredible dog breed.

Is the Siberian Husky breed well-liked in America?

The truth is that these dogs are very well-liked in America. Over the years they have become an increasingly popular dog breed.

How do people speak about the Siberian Husky?

People speak very highly about the Siberian Husky breed. They are often described as highly intelligent and lovable. They are seen as wonderful family dogs.

Has this breed starred in any movies?

There are a few movies which feature the Siberian Husky breed. Popular movies include Snow Buddies, Snow Dogs, Eight Below and the well-known movie Balto.

Are these dogs brave?

The Siberian Husky breed is known for its bravery. There are many of these dogs who are known as heroes. One famous dog who was a Siberian Husky was named Balto, he is well known in the history books for being a real-life dog hero.

Do these dogs have any unique physical features?

These dogs are known for a very unique physical feature. The name of this feature is called Heterochromia. This is when a Siberian Husky has one brown eye and one blue eye.

Are they an intelligent dog breed?

The truth is that the Siberian Husky is an incredibly smart dog breed. Their intelligence level is said to be the same as a two-year-old child.

Have Siberian Huskies ever worked in a war?

The answer is yes. Siberian Huskies have in fact worked in the war. They were used for multiple purposes. They were used for search and rescue and transportation purposes.

What is the ideal family for the Siberian Husky?

These dogs love company. The ideal family for the Siberian Husky is a family made up of a few humans, some dogs, and even some children. They love to play with children. The ideal family home will have lots of space and a big back garden.

Does the Siberian Husky need lots of grooming?

In comparison to other dog breeds, the Siberian Husky does not require as much grooming. They do require regular grooming just not as much as some other dogs.

How many years do they live up until?

On average the Siberian Husky dog lives around 12-15 years of age. This is a very average lifespan.

Do these dogs bark often?

In comparison to other dogs, the Siberian Husky does not bark that frequently. Although they are known to make howling noises.

Do they require lots of exercises?

The truth is that they do require lots of exercises. They can become extremely destructive if they are left alone for too long. They need regular exercise and lots of open space to run around.

What size are Siberian Huskies?

The Siberian Husky dog differs in size. For females, they usually weigh around 16-23 kg. Males usually weigh around 20-27kg. In terms of height, the females are around 50-56cm and males are 54-60cm.

What is the color of the Siberian Huskies eyes?

These dogs are known for their absolutely beautiful eyes. Their eyes can come in a few colors such as amber, brown or even blue.

What type of coats do Siberian Huskies have?

Siberian Husky dogs have a very thick and warm coat. It keeps them warm during the cold months. However, during the summer months, they can get very hot and have a tendency to overheat.

Which colors are these dogs?

These dogs usually come in a variety of colors. They can come in tan, black, white, copper and even grey. The most common color is white.

Which animal is associated with this dog breed?

Everyone all over the world compares the Siberian Husky to that of a wolf. All dogs are said to have descended from wolves. The Siberian Husky certainly also does come from the wolf.

Why were Siberian Huskies originally bred?

Siberian Huskies were originally bred in order to pull heavy objects. They were also used for herding animals and they were even used for being watchdogs. They were bred specifically for working purposes.

When did the breed first come to America?

From all the information that we have, it can be concluded that the first Siberian Husky came to America in 1908.

Where does the Siberian Husky breed come from?

The Siberian Husky dog breed originates all the way to Eastern Siberia. In case you were wondering, Siberia is situated in Russia.

Made in the USA
Monee, IL
26 July 2022

10376405R00026